This edition published by Parragon Books Ltd in 2018

Parragon Books Ltd
Chartist House
15–17 Trim Street
Bath BA1 1HA, UK
www.parragon.com

Designed by Lauren Tiley
Edited by Emma Horridge
Production by Jon Wakeham

ISBN 978-1-5270-1000-0

Printed in China

CONTENTS

ANIMALS

Why did the frog go to the hospital?
He needed a hop-eration.

What do you get when a cow has hiccups?
Milkshake.

What's a hedgehog's favourite food?
Prickled onions.

When is it bad luck to see a black cat?
When you are a mouse!

What do you call a rabbit's mobile home?
A wheel-burrow.

What happened to the shy tortoise?
He wouldn't come out of his shell.

Why did the pony cough?
Because he was a little horse.

What do you give a pig with a rash?
Oink-ment.

5

What do sloths throw in winter? Slowballs.

What do you give a sick canary? Medical tweetment.

What is it called when a cat wins a dog show? A cat-has-trophy.

Where do cows eat their lunch? At a calf-eteria.

What did the big weevil say to the little weevil? You're the lesser of two weevils.

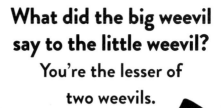

Why are elephants wrinkled? Have you ever tried to iron one?

What's a rabbit's favourite music? Hip-hop.

Why are a dog and a marine biologist alike? One wags a tail and the other tags a whale.

How did the bird break into the bank? With a crow bar.

What's small and cuddly and bright purple?
A koala holding its breath.

What did the snake's school report say?
His reading is poor but his writhing is excellent.

Where do pets go on holiday?
Hamster-dam.

What do rabbits do when they get married?
Go on bunnymoon.

Why do dogs wag their tails?
Because no one else will do it for them.

First cow: Moo.
Second cow: I was going to say that.

What do you call a pig who's rolling in cash?
Filthy rich.

What do you call a train driven by a snail?
A slow-comotive.

What do you call an elephant at the North Pole?
Lost.

What do you call a cheerful kangaroo?
A hop-timist.

How do you make a baby snake cry?
Take away its rattle.

What does a kitten become after it's three days old?
Four days old.

What dog can jump higher than a tree?
Any dog can jump higher than a tree, because trees can't jump.

What do you call a mouse that's three metres tall?
Enor-mouse.

What's the world's biggest insect?
A mam-moth.

How does a lion like his steak?
Medium roar.

15

Knock, knock.
Who's there?
Cows.
Cows who?
Cows moo, not who.

What do you call a camel with no humps?
Humphrey.

How do you save a drowning mouse?
Give it mouse-to-mouse resuscitation.

What did the woodworm say to the chair?
It's been nice gnawing you.

What does a lobster say when it answers the phone?
Shell-o?

What happened to the lion who turned into a cannibal?
He swallowed his pride.

Why couldn't the two elephants go swimming together?
Because they only had one pair of trunks.

What happens when ducks fly upside down?
They quack up.

What happened when Nelly the elephant ran away with the circus?
The police made her bring it back.

WRITE YOUR OWN JUNGLE JOKE...

How many sheep does it take to make a jumper? It depends how fast they can knit.

How do robins get in shape? They do worm-ups.

When do elephants have eight legs? When there are two of them.

What do you call a dog magician? A Labracadabrador.

What do you call
a fly with no wings?
A walk.

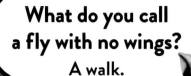

Why can't leopards hide?
Because they're
always spotted.

Which animal never stops talking?
A yak.

Why was the
pelican kicked
out of the hotel?
Because of his
huge bill.

What is brown, has a hump
and lives at the North Pole?
A very lost camel.

What is a crocodile's favourite game? Snap.

Where do you find giant snails? On the end of a giant's fingers.

Where did the silly woodworm live? In a brick.

What do monkeys do for laughs? They tell jokes about people.

Which insect makes films? Steven Spiel-bug.

What's worse than raining cats and dogs?
Hailing taxis.

What lies on its back with one hundred feet in the air?
A centipede having a nap.

Why don't elephants use computers?
They're too afraid of the mouse.

What has antlers and sucks blood?
A moose-quito!

21

How do fish
weigh themselves?
With their scales.

What's big
and grey and
puts everyone
into a trance?
A hypno-potamus.

What do elephants wear
under their trousers?
Ele-pants.

What do cows read to
their calves at bedtime?
Dairy tales.

22

What do you get if you cross a snake with a baker?

A pie-thon.

Why do fish live in salt water?

Because pepper makes them sneeze!

Why did the safari guide lose his driving licence?

He parked on a yellow lion.

What happens when a frog's car breaks down?

It gets toad away.

WRITE YOUR OWN ANIMAL JOKE...

What's worse
than a giraffe
with a stiff neck?
An elephant
with a cold.

Why are giraffes
so cheap to feed?
A little goes
a long way.

What do you get if
you cross a crocodile
with a camera?
A snapshot.

What do you get if you
cross a snake and a pig?
A boar constrictor.

What are the biggest ants in the world?

Gi-ants.

What are the second biggest ants in the world?

Eleph-ants.

What did the mouse say when it chipped its front teeth?

Hard cheese.

What do birds give out on Halloween?

Tweets.

25

What does a dog and a phone have in common? Collar ID.

What do you do when two snails have a fight? Leave them to slug it out.

What's the matter with hedgehogs? They won't share the hedge!

What has wings, a long tail and wears a bow? A birthday pheasant.

Why did the rhino go to the movies? She'd really enjoyed the book.

What should you do if a rhino charges? Pay up!

What musical instrument do mice play? The mouse organ.

What do you call a gorilla with bananas in its ears? Anything you like, it can't hear you!

Which fly has a sore throat? A hoarsefly.

What's grey and squirts jam at you? A mouse eating a doughnut.

Where do you find an upside-down turtle? Right where you left it!

What do you call a bee born in May? A maybe.

Why do rabbits eat rust? Because it's a type of car rot.

Why did the elephant leave the circus?
He'd had enough of working for peanuts.

How do snails get their shells so shiny?
They use snail varnish.

What's the difference between a fly and a mosquito?
A mosquito can fly, but a fly can't mosquito.

What do you call an alligator with a tummy bug?
An illigator.

WRITE YOUR OWN SNAPPY JOKE...

Where do baby monkeys sleep?
In ape-ricots.

Why did the baker stop making doughnuts?
Because he was tired of the hole business.

When should you feed giraffe milk to a baby?
When it's a baby giraffe.

Waiter, there's a fly swimming in my soup.
What do you expect me to do about it? Call a lifeguard?

What did the baby corn say to the mama corn?
Where's pop corn?

What did one plate say to the other?
Lunch is on me.

How did the elf get indigestion?
He kept goblin his dinner.

What did the lettuce say to the celery?
Stop stalking me!

What's a bear's favourite pasta?
Taglia-teddy.

Knock, knock.
Who's there?
Pete.
Pete who?
Pizza delivery man!

What do you get if you cross a prawn and a monkey?
A shrimp-anzee.

Customer: Waiter! I can't see any bananas in my banana surprise.
Waiter: I know, sir, that's the surprise.

What do you call cheese that doesn't belong to you?
Nacho cheese.

What do you call two banana skins?
A pair of slippers.

Waiter, there's a fly in my coffee.
That's all right, sir, he won't drink much.

What is a taxi driver's favourite food?
Corn on the cab.

Why did the bagel go to the dentist? Because it needed a filling.

What two things can you never have for breakfast? Lunch and dinner.

Knock, knock.
Who's there?
Noah.
Noah who?
Noah good burger bar round here?

A man who works in a butcher's shop is 6 feet tall and has size 11 feet. What does he weigh? Meat.

WRITE YOUR OWN CORNY JOKE...

Why are calendars sticky?
Because they're full of dates.

Why did the grape go out with a prune?
Because he couldn't get a date.

Waiter, there's a fly in my soup!
Don't worry, sir, the spider in your salad will eat it.

What's the difference between British ice cream and American ice cream?
About 5,000 kilometres.

Why are bells like oranges?
They peal.

What did the orange say to the banana?
You have a lot of a-peel.

Why did the farmer plough his field with a steamroller?
He wanted to grow mashed potatoes.

Why have you got a sausage behind your ear?
Oh dear, I must have eaten my pencil for lunch!

What cheese is made backwards? Edam.

What tricks do eggs play on each other? Practical yolks.

What's the fastest vegetable? The runner bean.

Knock knock.
Who's there?
Doughnut.
Doughnut who?
Doughnut ask, it's a secret.

What was purple and conquered the world? Alexander the Grape.

39

What is aggressive fruit good for?
Making fruit punch.

Why was the cafeteria's clock so slow?
It always went back four seconds.

Why did the grape stop in the middle of the road?
It ran out of juice.

Why are sausages bad-mannered?
Because they spit in the frying pan.

Knock knock.
Who's there?
Apple.
Apple who?
Apple.
Apple who??
Apple.
Apple who?!
Orange.
Orange who?
Orange you glad I didn't say apple?

What bird is with you at every meal?
A swallow.

Why don't you get hungry in a desert?
Because of all the sand-which-is there.

What does a mixed-up hen lay?
Scrambled eggs.

What does a refuse collector have for lunch?
Junk food.

What do you call a train full of toffees?
A chew-chew train.

What did the nut say when it sneezed?
Ca-shew!

Tom: What are you going to do with that horse manure?
Farmer: Put it on my strawberries.
Tom: Try cream and sugar – it tastes much better.

Mum: Why are you shivering?
Sam: Because you're making me chilli!

Knock, knock.
Who's there?
Ice cream.
Ice cream who?
Ice cream if you don't let me in!

What vegetable should you never have on a boat?
A leek.

How do you know carrots are good for your eyes?
Because you never see a rabbit wearing glasses.

If you divide an orange between six friends, what does each one get?
Sticky fingers.

Why was the boy staring at the juice carton?
Because it said 'concentrate'.

Why don't eggs tell jokes?
Because they would crack each other up.

Why did the teddy bear say no to dessert?
Because he was stuffed.

What did the leopard say after lunch?
That hit the spot!

What's purple and trapped in a tall tower?
A damson in distress.

Waiter, how often do you change the tablecloths in this restaurant?
I don't know, sir,
I've only been here six months.

What's the difference between a platypus and a pile of carrots?
One is a funny beast and the other is a bunny feast.

WRITE YOUR OWN TASTY JOKE...

Pancakes
by Mabel Syrup

Hard Cheese
by Ched Ar

Time to Eat
by Dean R. Bell

**Cooking for
Your Dog**
by Nora Bone

Perfect Pasta
by Al Dente

Breakfast Recipes
by Egon Toast

Quick Eats
by Mike Rowave

A Guide to Sausages
by Frank Furter

49

What did the angry customer give the chef at the Italian restaurant?

A pizza his mind.

Waiter, there's a worm on my plate.

No, sir, that's your sausage.

What's a pelican's favourite dish?

Anything that fits the bill.

Knock, knock.

Who's there?

Annie.

Annie who?

Annie more biscuits left? I'm starving!

What's green and wears an apron?

A cooking apple.

Why didn't the hot dog win an Oscar?
Because he didn't get any good rolls.

Customer: What do you call this?
Waiter: It's bean soup, sir.
Customer: I don't care what it's been, what is it now?

What's the easiest way to make a banana split?
Cut it in half.

WRITE YOUR OWN BANANAS JOKE...

Knock, knock.
Who's there?
Broccoli.
Broccoli who?
Don't be silly, broccoli doesn't have a last name.

What do you call stolen sweets?
Hot chocolate.

What do you get if you cross a chilli pepper, a spade and a Labrador?
A hot-diggity-dog.

Why did the cabbage win the race?
Because it was a-head.

What did the mayonnaise say when the fridge door opened?
Close the door, I'm dressing.

Why do seagulls fly over the sea?
Because if they flew over the bay they'd be bagels!

What are twins' favourite fruit?
Pears.

What do you get if you divide the circumference of a jack-o-lantern by its diameter?
Pumpkin pi.

What do you get from a pampered cow?
Spoiled milk.

What do you call a fake packet of spaghetti?

An im-pasta.

When is an Irish potato not an Irish potato?

When it's a French fry.

What came after the Stone Age and the Bronze Age?

The Saus-Age.

Why does cheese always look so sensible?

Because everything else on the plate is crackers.

Knock, knock.
Who's there?
Dishes.
Dishes who?
Dishes me, who are you?

What's a pumpkin's
favourite sport?
Squash.

How do you make
a sausage roll?
Push it down a hill.

What do you get if you cross a
chicken and a caterpillar?
Enough drumsticks for everyone.

Waiter!
There's a fly in my soup.
Don't worry, sir. It wiped its
feet on the bread roll.

Dentist:
Have your teeth
ever been checked?
Tom: No, they've always
been white.

Why are sports
arenas so windy?
Because of
all the fans.

Why did the lamp-post blush?
It saw the traffic light changing.

A thief broke into the police station and stole all the toilets. Police say they've got nothing to go on.

What colour is a hiccup? Burple.

What do you call a Roman emperor with a cold? Julius Sneezer.

Why shouldn't you swim on a full stomach? It's much easier swimming in a full swimming pool.

Why did the boy bring toilet paper to a party?
Because he was a party pooper.

Where does a bee sit?
On his bee-hind.

How did Mum know you hadn't washed?
I forgot to wet the towel!

Are those croissants I smell?
Yes, and you do.

What do you call a bathroom superhero?
Flush Gordon.

What happens if you play table tennis with a bad egg?
First it goes ping, then it goes pong.

You had egg for breakfast, I can see it on your chin.
No I didn't, that was yesterday.

What are you if you step in a cow pat?
An incowpoop.

What happens if you pee on the toilet seat?
Urine big trouble.

Where do monkeys buy their underpants?
At a jungle sale.

What do you call a man with a bogey problem?
No one nose.

What did the tissue say to the nose?
Don't get snotty with me!

Waiter! This fish smells terrible. Unfortunately, it's a case of long time, no sea.

Why did the skunk need a tissue? Because it had a stinking cold.

Two fleas were on their way into town. 'Shall we walk?' asked one. 'No,' said the second. 'Let's take a dog.'

Puns about toilet paper are usually just tear-able.

How do you cook toilet paper? Just throw it in the pot.

What did the bath say to the toilet? You look a bit flushed.

Did you hear about the skunk that went into space? It stunk to high heaven.

What do you get if you eat a lot of alphabet soup? A big vowel movement.

Waiter! Why have you got your thumb on my apple pie? To stop it falling on the floor again, madam.

Your dog's really lazy.
Why do you say that?
Yesterday I watered the garden and he never lifted a leg to help me.

Knock, knock.
Who's there?
Stan.
Stan who?
Stan back, I'm going to sneeze!

What's the difference between a wolf and a flea?
One howls on the prairie and the other prowls on the hairy.

WRITE YOUR OWN GROSS JOKE...

What happened to the snake with a cold?
She adder viper nose.

What's brown and sounds like a bell?
Dung.

What's an ig?
An ice house without a loo.

What's black, gushes out of the ground and shouts, 'Knickers!'?
Crude oil.

What has four legs and flies?
A dead sheep.

Mum: Stop picking your nose!
Boy: Why? Snot fair!

Why did the frog cross the road?
To show his friend he had guts.

What's black, gushes out of the ground and shouts, 'I beg your pardon!'?
Refined oil.

What's the difference between bogeys and cabbage?
Kids don't eat cabbage.

What did the nose say to the boy?
Why are you always picking on me?

Did you hear the story about the dustbin lorry?
It was a load of old rubbish.

What happened when the scientist swallowed uranium?
He got atomic ache.

What's the difference between a toilet brush and a biscuit?
You can't dip a toilet brush in your tea.

What do skunks sing at Christmas?
Jingle Smells.

How many farts does it take to make a stink bomb?
A phew.

That film gave me a cold, slithery feeling down the back of my neck.
So that's where my ice cream went!

Common Cold Symptoms
by Ronnie Nose

Mud, Snot and Slime
by S. Platt

Ouch!
by A. B. Stung

Sneezing Fit
by A. Chew

Living on Garlic and Onions
by I. Malone

Introduction to Dentistry
by
Phil McCavity

Garden Full of Weeds?
by
Dan D. Lyon

Did you hear about the dog that ate garlic? Its bark was worse than its bite.

What do you get if you poo in your overalls? Dung-arees.

What do you call a man with a toilet on his head? Lou.

Why can't a steam engine sit down? Because it has a tender behind.

How do you catch dandruff? Shake your head over a paper bag.

72

What's soft, mouldy and flies around at night?
A spoiled bat.

Where's the best place to have the school sickroom?
Next to the canteen!

Knock, knock.
Who's there?
Ahab.
Ahab who?
Ahab to go to the toilet in a hurry!

What's the smelliest city in the United States?
Phew York.

Why do giraffes have such long necks? Because their feet smell.

What's brown, hairy and full of snot? A coconut with a cold.

What has bottom at the top? Your legs.

Why are skunks always fighting? They like to raise a stink.

What does a spider wear to get married?
A webbing dress.

What has four wheels and goes 'Hic! Hic! Hic!'?
A hiccup truck.

Did you hear what happened to the flea circus?
A dog came along and stole the show!

Did you hear the joke about the smelly t-shirt?
That one's on you!

WRITE YOUR OWN SNOTTY JOKE...

MONSTERS

Why was the werewolf arrested in the butcher's shop?
He was chop-lifting.

How do monsters communicate?
By terror-phone.

Which monster sits on the end of your finger?
The bogeyman.

Why do witches wear name tags?
So they know which witch is which.

What does a ghost do to stay safe in the car?
Puts on a sheet belt.

Where do ghost trains stop?
At devil crossings.

What do witches put on their hair?
Scare spray.

What do you get if King Kong sits on your piano?
A flat note.

79

What is a vampire's favourite type of boat?
Blood vessels.

What do you get if you cross a vampire and a teacher?
Lots of blood tests.

What kind of plate does a skeleton eat his dinner from?
Bone china.

What's a skeleton's favourite type of joke?
A rib-tickler.

What position did the ghost play in the football team?
Ghoul-keeper.

Jack: There's a monster at the door with a really funny face.
Dad: Tell him you've already got one.

Why does everyone hate Dracula?
Because he's a pain in the neck.

What would you get if you crossed Halloween with April 1st?
April Ghouls' Day.

WRITE YOUR OWN SCARY JOKE...

Why did the witch buy a new computer? Because it had a spell checker.

Why are mummies the most selfish monsters? Because they are all wrapped up in themselves.

What do you do if you want to learn more about Dracula? Join his fang club.

What does a mummy say when it hears a terrible joke? That sphinx!

What should you do if you find a monster under your bed?
Find somewhere else to sleep.

What do you call an angry monster?
Sir!

What do you call a skeleton that won't get out of bed?
Lazy Bones.

What's a ghost's favourite dessert?
I scream.

Where do vampires keep their savings?
In the blood bank.

Did you hear about the werewolf who lost his voice?
He's howl right now.

Mummy, everyone says I look like a werewolf.
Be quiet and comb your face.

What do ghosts eat with roast beef?
Grave-y.

Why don't ghosts like rain?
It dampens their spirits.

What kind of music do mummies listen to?
Wrap.

Why do witches think they're funny?
Every time they look in the mirror, it cracks up.

What does a vampire take for a bad cold?
Coffin drops.

85

Why did the vampire's lunch give her heartburn?
It was a stake sandwich.

Why was the mummy so tense?
He was all wound up.

What only goes out at night and goes chomp, suck, ouch?
A vampire with a rotten fang.

Knock, knock.
Who's there?
Boo.
Boo who?
Don't cry, it's only a knock-knock joke!

Where does a ghost go on Saturday night? Anywhere she can boo-gie.

Why did the festering zombie stay in bed? He felt rotten.

Why do vampires have chickpeas, lentils and beans with their meals? Because they'll eat anything with pulses.

What do you say to a three-headed monster? Hello, hello, hello!

What do you call a corpse with nothing to do?
Bored stiff.

Why do vampires drink blood?
Because coffee keeps them awake all day!

Why did the vampire need mouthwash?
She had bat breath.

Why is Frankenstein such good fun?
Because he'll have you in stitches.

WRITE YOUR OWN MONSTER JOKE...

What do you get if you cross a cat with a lemon?
A sour puss.

Which instrument does a skeleton play?
A trombone.

Knock, knock.
Who's there?
Donna.
Donna who?
Donna look now, but there's a big monster right behind you!

Why couldn't the witch give a speech?
She had a frog in her throat.

What did the skeleton
weather forecaster say?
Tomorrow's weather
will be bone dry.

What is as sharp as
a vampire's fang?
His other fang.

Why did the
vampires cancel
their baseball game?
They couldn't find
their bats.

What do monsters
sing at Christmas?
Deck the halls with poison ivy!

What game did the ghosts play at the party?
Hide and shriek.

Why did the monster ask to leave the table?
He'd already eaten the fridge, the stove and the kitchen cabinets.

What do you call a ghost that plays football?
Team spirit.

Why did the skeleton go to the party?
To have a rattling good time.

What do you call a vampire that's always feeling peckish?
Snackula.

Where do spirits post their letters?
At the ghost office.

What did the rude ghost say to the vampire?
So long, sucker!

Why are monsters so clever?
Because two heads are better than one.

Why did the sorceress have a huge mansion? Because she was so witch.

Why did the witch wash her broomstick? She wanted to make a clean sweep of it.

Why didn't the skeleton get a job? He was bone idle.

What do you get when you cross a chicken with a ghost? A poultry-geist.

WRITE YOUR OWN SPOOKY JOKE...

Where do Martians get their eggs? From the little green hen.

What do you call a witch who lives by the beach but is frightened of the sea? A chicken sand-witch.

What kind of dog does Dracula have? A bloodhound.

What do monsters have on their toast? Scream cheese.

What's a vampire's favourite celebration? Fangs-giving.

Why didn't the skeleton enjoy work? His heart wasn't in it.

What did the skeleton say while riding his motorbike? I'm bone to be wild!

What kind of
hot dogs do monsters
like best?
Hallowieners!

Why couldn't the witch
fly for long distances?
She got broomsick.

What do you
call a rich elf?
Welfy.

What should you say when you meet a ghost?
Hello, how do you boo?

Where do zombies eat lunch?
At the cadaver-teria.

Why did the wizard get into the fridge?
There was a cold spell coming.

What's the best way to imagine you're flying on a broomstick?
Witchful thinking.

What do witches take to the beach?
Suntan potion.

What did the witch teacher do to the badly behaved student?
Ex-spelled her.

What's the best pet for a ghost?
A scaredy cat.

What do you call a mysterious wizard on a broomstick?
An unidentified flying sorcerer.

Why can't skeletons play music in church?
They don't have organs.

When does a ghost have breakfast?
In the moaning.

What instrument do Hawaiian ghosts play?
The spook-ulele.

What story do little ghosts like to hear at bedtime?
Ghoul-dilocks and the Three Scares.

What is a ghost's favourite dessert?
Boo-berry pie.

Knock, knock.
Who's there?
Philip.
Philip who?
Philip my bag with sweets, I'm trick-or-treating!

What do you get
if you cross a monster
with a pig?
Frankenswine.

What's spotty, scary,
and has 16 wheels?
A monster on
roller skates.

LOL

What musical instrument do you pick up every morning?
A tuba toothpaste.

Why did the girl eat yeast and shoe polish?
So that she'd rise and shine every day.

What does a tortoise do on its birthday?
It shellebrates.

Who made King Arthur's Round Table?
Sir Cumference.

Why did the one-armed man cross the road?
To get to the second-hand shop.

Customer: Can I try on that dress in the window?
Shop assistant: No, you'll have to use the changing room!

What did the scarf say to the hat?
You go on ahead and I'll hang around.

Patient: Doctor, I feel as though I'm invisible.
Doctor: Who said that?

Why did the seahorse get a promotion?
Because he was so e-fish-ent.

Why did Robin Hood only rob the rich?
Because the poor didn't have much to steal.

Why did the burglar take the legs off his bed?
He wanted to lie low.

What did the policeman say to his belly button?
You're under a vest.

What happened to the
first restaurant on the moon?
The food was good, but the
place lacked atmosphere.

Where did the
broken doll go
to get fixed?
To the
plastic surgeon.

What happened when
Bluebeard fell into the Red Sea?
He was marooned.

What keeps
rock stars cool?
Their fans.

Where did the astronaut leave her spaceship?
At a parking meteor.

What do angry rodents send each other at Christmas?
Cross mouse cards.

What did the alien say to the chef?
Take me to your larder.

Who drives all his customers away but still makes a living?
A taxi driver.

When's the best time to visit the dentist? Two thirty.

What do you call Stone Age jokes? Pre-hysterical.

What happened to the robber who fell into a cement mixer? He became a hardened criminal.

Did you hear about the man who tried to cross the Atlantic on a plank of wood? He couldn't find one long enough.

WRITE YOUR OWN WHACKY JOKE...

Teacher: What do you find at the end of a rainbow?

Callum: The letter 'W'.

Teacher: You weren't at school yesterday, Alex. I heard you were at the cinema.

Alex: That's not true – I've got the tickets from the football match to prove it!

Teacher: You should have been here at 9 o'clock.

Tom: Why, did something exciting happen?

Why did the boy eat his homework?

Because the teacher told him it was a piece of cake.

Teacher: What was the Romans' most remarkable achievement?
Ellie: Learning Latin!

Teacher: Why are you always late for school?
Matthew: Because you always ring the bell before I get here!

Why did the kid walk backwards to school?
It was back-to-school day.

Teacher: 'This essay about your pet parrot is exactly the same as the one your sister handed in!'
Amelia: Yes, Miss, it's the same parrot.

Why did the doctor lose her temper? Because she'd run out of patients.

Why did the bald man stick his head out of the window? To get some fresh hair.

What do you call Australian boxer shorts? Down-underwear.

How do you stop an astronaut's baby from crying? Rocket.

How do you make a pirate angry? Take away the 'p'.

Why did the boy's gran knit him three socks?
Because he had grown another foot.

What did the bookworm say to the librarian?
Can I burrow this book, please?

Knock, knock.
Who's there?
Woo!
Whoo who?
Don't get too excited, it's just a knock, knock joke.

Mum: Did you know that most accidents happen in the kitchen?
Sophie: Yes, and I have to eat them!

Why are aliens good at gardening?
Because they have green fingers.

What has two legs,
a mop and flies?
A caretaker covered in jam.

What kind of driver
doesn't need a licence?
A screwdriver.

What do you call
an underwater spy?
James Pond.

What makes a good librarian? Shelf control.

Dad: What's on the TV? Sam: A bowl of fruit and a vase.

Uncle Dave: You're very quiet, Joe. Joe: Well, Mum told me to not say anything about your massive nose.

Where do knights have dinner? In an all-knight diner.

What do you get if you cross a UFO with a rasher of bacon?

A frying saucer.

Mum: Why did you put a mouse in Auntie's bed?

George: Because I couldn't find a spider.

What should you do if you break your leg in two places?

Stay away from those places in future.

Why do bakers work late?

Because they knead the dough.

What goes in pink and comes out blue?
A swimmer on a cold day.

Ryan: How did you get that black eye?
Jamie: You see that tree in the playground?
Ryan: Yes.
Jamie: Well, I didn't.

What happened to the robber who broke into the soap factory?
He made a clean getaway.

WRITE YOUR OWN LOL JOKE...

Teacher: Are you good at arithmetic?

Nathan: Well, yes and no.

Teacher: What do you mean, yes and no?

Nathan: Yes, I'm no good at arithmetic.

Holly: Why are you going to night school?

Heidi: To learn how to read in the dark!

George: My teacher gave me a detention for something I didn't do!

Mum: That's terrible! What didn't you do?

George: My homework.

Where do ghosts do their homework?
Exorcise books.

Why was the maths book unhappy?
Because it had loads of problems.

What did the alien say to the school librarian?
Take me to your reader.

Mum: What did you learn in school today?
Will: How to write.
Mum: What did you write?
Will: I don't know, they haven't taught us how to read yet!

Jake: Somebody threw a stink bomb into the boys' toilets today.
Mum: How did it smell?
Jake: Much better!

Why do short chefs have problems at work?
The steaks are too high.

Why did the scarecrow win an award?
Because he was the best in his field.

What part of a car sleeps the most?
The wheels – they're always tired!

Why are pirates called pirates?
They just arrrrr.

120

What does a dentist call her x-rays?
Tooth pics.

Why was the musician arrested?
He was always getting into treble.

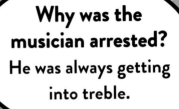

What did the Martian chef find in his cupboard?
An unidentified frying object.

Why are orchestras so badly behaved?
They don't know how to conduct themselves.

WRITE YOUR OWN SIDE-SPLITTING JOKE...

The Millionaire
by Ivor Fortune

**The
100 Yard Dash**
by Willie Makit
*Illustrated by
Betty Wont*

**Teach Your
Parrot to Talk**
by L. O. Polly

122

Why didn't people send birthday cards in the Stone Age?
The stamps wouldn't stick to the rocks.

Why did the boy throw the clock out of the window?
He wanted to see time fly.

What do history teachers do for fun?
They talk about old times.

Where do astronauts keep their sandwiches?
In a launch box.

WRITE YOUR OWN HYSTERICAL JOKE...

Dad: Where's your school report?
Ben: My mate borrowed it.
He wanted to scare his parents.

Why did the
teacher wear sunglasses?
Because her class was so bright.

Knock, knock.
Who's there?
Scott.
Scott who?
Scott nothing
to do with you!

Who tells
chicken jokes?
Comedi-hens.